B L
3.2

First Facts®

Christmas around the World

Christmas in
FRANCE

by Jack Manning

CAPSTONE PRESS
a capstone imprint

First Facts are published by Capstone Press,
1710 Roe Crest Drive, North Mankato, Minnesota 56003
www.capstonepub.com

Library of Congress Cataloging-in-Publication Data
Manning, Jack.
  Christmas in France / by Jack Manning.
     pages cm.—(First facts: Christmas around the world)
  Includes index.
  ISBN 978-1-4765-3102-1 (library binding)
  ISBN 978-1-4765-3433-6 (ebook PDF)
1. Christmas—France—Juvenile literature. 2. France—Social life and customs—Juvenile literature.
I. Title.
  GT4987.48.M34 2014
  394.26630944—dc23   2013003484

Editorial Credits
Brenda Haugen, editor; Gene Bentdahl, designer; Eric Gohl, media researcher;
Jennifer Walker, production specialist

Photo Credits
Capstone Studio: Karon Dubke, 21; Dreamstime: Claudio Momberto, 6, Giancarlo Liguori, 5;
Fotolia: Marco Desscouleurs, 1; Newscom: Godong/picture-alliance/Fred de Noyelle, 11, 17,
PHOTOPQR/L'UNION DE REIMS/Christian Philippe, 15, ZUMA Press/Colorise/Risler, 12,
ZUMA Press/Stephane Geufroi, 20; Shutterstock: pearl7, 18; Super Stock Inc.: Photononstop,
cover, 8

Design Elements: Shutterstock

Printed in China by Nordica.
0413/CA21300423
032013   007226NORDF13

TABLE OF CONTENTS

Christmas in France

People sing songs. Flowers fill homes with color. Children write letters asking for gifts. These are some of the sights and sounds of Christmas in France. People celebrate Christmas Day on December 25. But the Christmas season lasts much longer. It begins December 6 with the feast of Saint Nicholas. Christmas celebrations end January 6 with Epiphany.

How to Say It!

In France people say "*Joyeux Noël*" (jwah-YEUH no-EL), which means "Happy Christmas."

France

5

CHRISTMAS FACT!

Three kings followed a star to the stable where Jesus was born. The kings brought gifts for Jesus. Epiphany celebrates the day the three kings first saw Jesus.

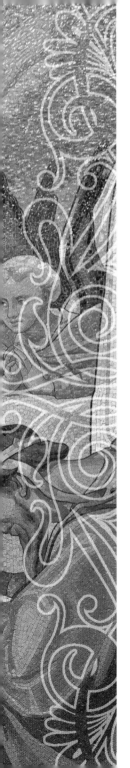

The First Christmas

Christmas is a **Christian** holiday that celebrates the birth of **Jesus**. Long ago Mary and Joseph traveled to the city of Bethlehem. The city is in the Middle East. Mary was going to have a baby. When Mary and Joseph got to the city, they had no place to stay. They spent the night in a stable. Jesus was born there.

Christian—a person who follows a religion based on the teachings of Jesus
Jesus—the founder of the Christian religion

Christmas Celebrations

The Christmas season is full of celebrations. The feast of Saint Nicholas starts the season. Saint Nicholas helped poor children. On his feast day, children often receive candy or other treats.

Most people celebrate on Christmas Eve. They go to midnight church services. A meal called *réveillon* (reh-vay-OHN) follows the services. Réveillon means to wake up.

The last day of the Christmas season is Epiphany, Three Kings Day. Many people go to church on Epiphany. They also eat a special treat called the Cake of Kings.

Christmas Symbols

The crèche (KRESH) is a symbol of Christmas. It is a scene that reminds people of Jesus' birth.

Many crèches include small figures called *santons* (sahn-TOHNZ). Most santons look like people or animals. Some are of Jesus, Mary, and Joseph. Others are shaped like the three kings.

CHRISTMAS FACT!

Santons are made from hard, waterproof clay. Many people paint the santons by hand.

Christmas Decorations

Flowers decorate many tables during the Christmas season. Roses, carnations, and snapdragons are popular choices.

More people decorate with Christmas trees than in the past. They sometimes use potted trees. They often plant the trees outside after the Christmas season.

People put **ornaments** and lights on their Christmas trees. Common ornaments include balls, bells, and angels.

ornament—a decoration hung on a Christmas tree

Santa Claus

Most French children believe in Père Noël (PEHR no-EL), which means Father Christmas. Père Noël is a tall man with a white beard. He wears a long, red robe. He carries a sack of gifts for children.

Children write letters to Père Noël at the North Pole. In the letters, children politely ask for gifts.

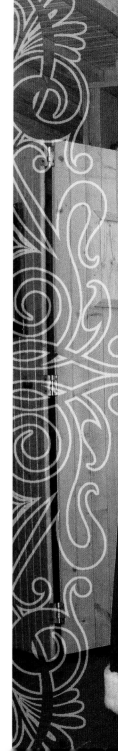

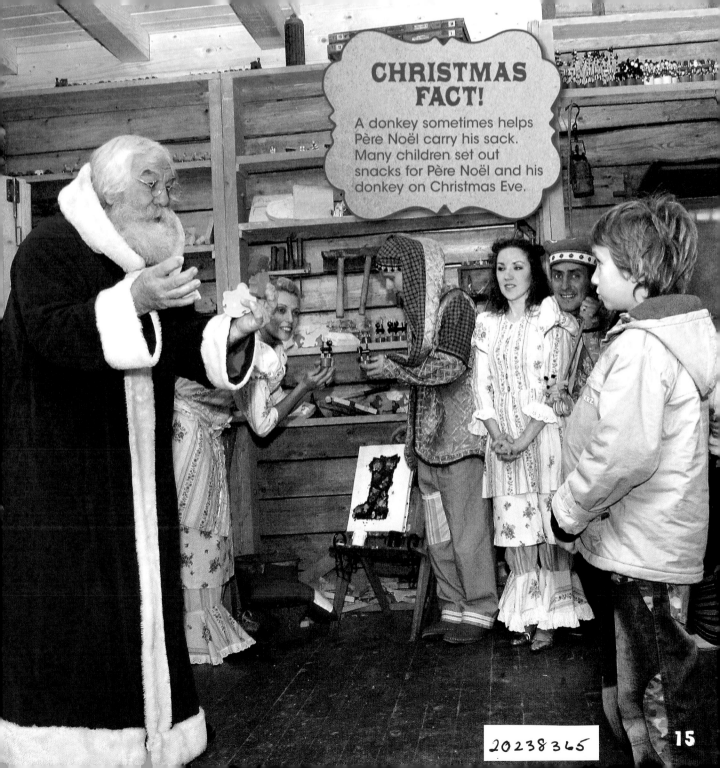

20238365

Christmas Presents

Some people believe Père Noël comes twice. He brings small gifts and candy for children on the feast of Saint Nicholas. Père Noël also comes on Christmas Eve.

Some children put their shoes near the fireplace on Christmas Eve. Others put their shoes near the crèche or the Christmas tree. They hope Père Noël will fill them with presents.

Children open their gifts on Christmas Day. Adults open their gifts on January 1, which is New Year's Day. Most children receive toys, games, and candy.

CHRISTMAS FACT!

Many people give gifts to community helpers, such as butchers or letter carriers.

Christmas Food

On Christmas Eve families gather around tables filled with food. They eat small helpings from the many dishes. The meal may last for hours.

People eat many kinds of foods during the Christmas season. Some eat roasted goose. Others eat turkey and chestnuts. **Oysters** are a favorite Christmas food in Paris, the capital of France.

oyster—a flat shellfish

Christmas Songs

Christmas in France is a joyful time filled with music. One famous Christmas song from France is "Oh, Holy Night."

Many people celebrate Christmas with musical shows. The shows are held in churches, concert halls, and theaters.

Christmas show in France

CHRISTMAS FACT!

Placide Cappeau wrote the words to "Oh, Holy Night" in 1847. He was a sales person and mayor of Roquemaure.

Hands-On:
MAKE A KING

The three kings came to a Bethlehem stable to see the baby Jesus. Now you can make your own king to decorate your home.

What You Need

- construction paper in several colors
- glue
- scissors
- colored pencils or markers

What You Do

1. Roll a sheet of construction paper into a tube, and glue it in place.
2. After the glue dries, cut out two squares about 1 inch (2.5 centimeters) high on opposite sides of the bottom of the tube. These cutouts will form the king's legs.
3. Make the king's face from a strip of construction paper that is a different color from the tube. Use colored pencils or markers to draw the king's eyes, nose, and mouth. Glue the face around the top of the tube.
4. Create a beard by cutting slits along the bottom edge of another strip of construction paper. Glue the beard to the tube beneath the face.
5. Make a crown for your king with another strip of construction paper. Cut points along the top of the paper to make the crown. Then glue the crown in place.
6. Decorate your king. You can add cutouts or draw designs on your king and his crown.

GLOSSARY

Christian (KRIS-chuhn)—a person who follows a religion based on the teachings of Jesus

Jesus (JEE-zuhs)—the founder of the Christian religion; Christians believe that Jesus is the son of God

ornament (OR-nuh-muhnt)—a decoration hung on a Christmas tree

oyster (OY-stur)—a flat shellfish

READ MORE

Alcraft, Rob. *A Visit to France.* Chicago: Heinemann Library, 2008.

Farmer, Jacqueline. *O Christmas Tree: Its History and Holiday Traditions.* Watertown, Mass.: Charlesbridge, 2010.

Trunkhill, Brenda. *Christmas around the World.* St. Louis: Concordia Publishing House, 2009.

INTERNET SITES

FactHound offers a safe, fun way to find Internet sites related to this book. All of the sites on FactHound have been researched by our staff.

Here's all you do:

Visit *www.facthound.com*

Type in this code: 9781476531021

Check out projects, games and lots more at
www.capstonekids.com

INDEX